Italian
CUISINE

Enslow PUBLISHING

BY JENNIFER LOMBARDO

COOKING WITH CULTURE

Please visit our website, www.enslow.com. For a free color catalog of all our high-quality books, call toll free 1-800-398-2504 or fax 1-877-980-4454.

Library of Congress Cataloging-in-Publication Data
Names: Lombardo, Jennifer, author.
Title: Italian cuisine / Jennifer Lombardo.
Description: Buffalo, New York : Enslow Publishing, 2025. | Series: Cooking with culture | Includes index.
Identifiers: LCCN 2024002715 | ISBN 9781978540422 (library binding) | ISBN 9781978540415 (paperback) | ISBN 9781978540439 (ebook)
Subjects: LCSH: Cooking, Italian–Juvenile literature. | Food–Italy–History–Juvenile literature | LCGFT: Cookbooks.
Classification: LCC TX723 .L586 2025 | DDC 641.5945–dc23/eng/20240212
LC record available at https://lccn.loc.gov/2024002715

Published in 2025 by
Enslow Publishing
2544 Clinton Street
Buffalo, NY 14224

Copyright © 2025 Enslow Publishing

Portions of this work were originally authored by John Matthew and published as *Foods of Italy*. All new material in this edition authored by Jennifer Lombardo.

Designer: Leslie Taylor
Editor: Caitie McAneney

Photo credits: Cover (photo) etaruscas/Shutterstock.com; Series Art (background icon pattern) porcelaniq/Shutterstock.com; Series Art (series logo) lukeruk/Shutterstock.com; p. 5 leoks/Shutterstock.com; p. 7 Elegant Solution/Shutterstock.com; p. 9 Andrii Shnaider/Shutterstock.com; p. 11 leoks/Shutterstock.com; p. 13 UliAb/Shutterstock.com; p. 15 Micaela Fiorellini/Shutterstock.com; p. 17 smspsy/Shutterstock.com; p. 19 Brent Hofacker/Shutterstock.com; p. 21 (biscotti) Katty S/Shutterstock.com, (gelato) JM Travel Photography/Shutterstock.com, (cannoli) Harmony Waldron/Shutterstock.com, (tiramisu) Alena_Kos/Shutterstock.com.

All rights reserved. No part of this book may be reproduced in any form without permission in writing from the publisher, except by a reviewer.

Some of the images in this book illustrate individuals who are models. The depictions do not imply actual situations or events.

Printed in the United States of America

CPSIA compliance information: Batch #CSENS25: For further information contact Enslow Publishing at 1-800-398-2504.

Contents

Eating Around Italy 4
A Perfect Pairing 6
Fresh Food 8
Exploring the North 10
Central Cuisine 12
When in Rome 14
Pass the Pizza! 16
A Sample from Sicily 18
Delicious Desserts 20
Recipe: Biscotti 21
Glossary 22
For More Information 23
Index 24

Words in the glossary appear in **bold** type the first time they are used in the text.

Eating Around Italy

Italy is a country full of mountains, hills, and stunning coastlines. Its food is as **diverse** as its landscapes! In fact, these landscapes sometimes made it hard for people to travel before modern roads. That means different **regions** often had different foods.

FOOD FOR THOUGHT

ITALY HAS ABOUT 4,722 MILES (7,599 KM) OF COASTLINE. THAT MEANS THERE ARE A LOT OF SEAFOOD DISHES IN ITALIAN **CULTURE**.

Seafood is popular in coastal towns. Cioppino is a popular Italian seafood stew.

While you may be most familiar with pizza and pasta, there are many different Italian foods to explore! Many people visit Italy to taste the yummy foods the country has to offer. In this book, you'll get a taste for the **specialties** of Italy.

A Perfect Pairing

Pasta is one of the most popular Italian foods eaten around the world. It has a long history! Records from around 100 CE report that Romans baked wheat noodles in ovens. Today, pasta in Italy is boiled in water.

Pasta is often eaten with tomato sauce. However, this wasn't a popular pairing until the 1800s. That's because tomatoes didn't grow in Italy. Explorers brought tomatoes to Europe from North America in the 1500s. However, many Italians thought these strange red fruits might be harmful!

FOOD FOR THOUGHT

NOODLES MADE 4,000 YEARS AGO HAVE BEEN FOUND IN CHINA.

Some kinds of pasta are long and thin, like spaghetti. Some are short and round, like orecchiette.

Fresh Food

The landscape and soil of Italy makes it easy to grow many fresh fruits and vegetables. That's why fresh **ingredients** are so important to Italian dishes.

Olive trees and tomatoes grow well in Italy. The Italian word for tomato is *pomodoro*.

FOOD FOR THOUGHT

BECAUSE PASTA IS SO POPULAR, ITALY GROWS AND **IMPORTS** WHEAT FROM OTHER COUNTRIES. MOST ITALIANS EAT ABOUT 50 POUNDS (23 KG) OF PASTA YEARLY!

To use fresh ingredients, Italians look at what foods are in season at the market.

The exact meaning of pomodoro is "apple of gold." Olive oil is just as important to Italian food as tomatoes. Other fresh foods used in Italian cooking include eggplants, zucchini, peppers, and melons.

Exploring the North

Northern Italy has its own special **cuisine**. In Lombardy, a region of northern Italy, risotto is a popular dish. Risotto is a dish made of a small kind of rice. **Polenta** is another popular grain. Meats, such as chicken, are coated with breadcrumbs and fried. Dishes cooked this way are called Milanese, after the region's capital city of Milan.

Venice is a city that sits on top of many islands. There's water all around!

To the east of Lombardy, the Veneto region touches the Adriatic Sea. In its capital city of Venice, you can find many seafood dishes with scallops, squid, mussels, and more.

FOOD FOR THOUGHT

PROSCIUTTO IS A THIN, SEASONED HAM THAT'S MADE IN A REGION OF NORTHERN ITALY. TO MAKE IT, PORK MEAT IS COVERED IN SALT AND LEFT OUT FOR WEEKS.

Central Cuisine

Central Italy is home to the regions of Tuscany and Umbria. In Tuscany, common ingredients include fresh olives, homemade cheese, and fresh **herbs**. Soups made with beans are also popular. Its capital, Florence, has many specialties. The phrase *alla Fiorentina* means "in the style of Florence." *Bistecca alla Fiorentina* is a **recipe** for high-quality beef served rare, or just lightly cooked.

FOOD FOR THOUGHT

PAPPARDELLE IS A KIND OF TUSCAN PASTA OFTEN MADE WITH EGGS IN THE **DOUGH** FOR A RICH TASTE.

pappardelle pasta with black truffles

Many fresh foods can be found in Tuscany, including special mushrooms called truffles.

Some of the Umbria region's mouthwatering dishes are made with gnocchi (NOH-kee), which are potato **dumplings**. Gnocchi are often served with sauce and cheeses.

13

When in Rome

Central Italy is home to the famous city of Rome. One popular dish is *pasta arrabbiata*, which is spicy. Pasta carbonara is made with eggs, pork, and cheese. Perhaps the most well-known dish is bruschetta. Bruschetta are thick slices of bread that are toasted, rubbed with garlic, and sprinkled with olive oil and salt. Sometimes tomatoes are placed on top.

FOOD FOR THOUGHT

SPICES SUCH AS BLACK PEPPER AND HOT PEPPERS ARE USED IN MANY ROMAN DISHES TO PROVIDE SPICY OR SMOKY TASTES.

One of the most famous pasta dishes in Rome is *cacio e pepe*. "Cacio" is a kind of cheese, and "pepe" means black pepper.

Artichokes are a commonly used vegetable in Italy. Artichokes prepared *alla Romana* (or "Roman style") are cooked in oil, garlic, and parsley.

Pass the Pizza!

Many people think of Italy when they think of pizza. For hundreds of years, different cultures around the world have been making flatbreads and putting oil and herbs on them. However, modern pizza began in the city of Naples in the southern region of Campania.

FOOD FOR THOUGHT

NEAPOLITAN PIZZA HAS THE SAME COLORS AS THE ITALIAN FLAG: GREEN BASIL, WHITE CHEESE, AND RED TOMATOES.

Real Neapolitan pizza uses San Marzano tomatoes and buffalo mozzarella cheese.

In 1889, the people of Naples, called Neapolitans, wanted to prepare something special for their visiting queen, named Margherita. This Neapolitan pizza, also called a margherita pizza, was the first modern pizza.

A Sample from Sicily

Many people think Italy looks like a boot, and there's a little island that's near the toe. It's called Sicily, and it has its own special foods.

Before you eat a Sicilian meal, you may have antipasto. Antipasto means "before the meal." It may include meats, cheeses, vegetables, or any other food.

arancini

Arancini has been made for over 1,000 years!

Another common Sicilian dish is arancini. It consists of balls of rice and meat coated in breadcrumbs and fried. It is a staple food in Sicily!

FOOD FOR THOUGHT

MANY DIFFERENT PEOPLES HAVE OCCUPIED SICILY OVER THE YEARS, INCLUDING GREEKS, SPANIARDS, ARABS, AND EVEN VIKINGS. EACH GROUP LEFT BEHIND A BIT OF ITS OWN CUISINE.

Delicious Desserts

When a good Italian meal is over, it's time for a tasty treat. Many Italians enjoy gelato, a kind of rich ice cream. You can find gelato in many different flavors. It's the perfect dessert for a hot day.

Cannoli are pastries stuffed with sweet cheese. Italian cookies include biscotti, *cuccidati*, and amaretti. Italian bakeries, called *panetteria*, often have many sweet treats for people to buy. As with all Italian foods, each region and baker may have their own special recipe to share.

FOOD FOR THOUGHT

BISCOTTI ARE POPULAR COOKIES THAT ARE BAKED TWICE. ROMAN SOLDIERS ATE BISCOTTI OVER 2,000 YEARS AGO!

Biscotti

biscotti

Ingredients
- 10 tablespoons softened unsalted butter
- 1 1/3 cups sugar
- 3 large eggs
- 2 teaspoons vanilla extract
- 3 1/4 cups flour
- 1 tablespoon baking powder
- 3/4 teaspoon salt
- 2/3 cup mini chocolate chips

Tiramisu is an Italian dessert with a sweet coffee taste.

Equipment
- stand mixer or hand mixer
- knife
- cookie sheet
- parchment paper
- measuring cups and spoons
- two mixing bowls

Steps
1. Preheat oven to 350°F (175°C).
2. Put parchment paper on a cookie sheet.
3. Beat butter and sugar together using a mixer.
4. Add eggs one at a time. Stir.
5. Stir in vanilla extract.
6. In a separate bowl, combine flour, salt, and baking powder.
7. Add the flour mixture to the butter mixture a little bit at a time while stirring.
8. Add in mini chocolate chips.
9. Form dough into two separate logs about 10 inches long and 2 inches wide, spaced 4 inches apart.
10. Bake for 30 minutes. Cookies should look golden brown. Let them cool.
11. Use a knife to slice the logs into slices about 1 1/2 inches thick and place them face down on the cookie sheet.
12. Bake the biscotti for 10 more minutes on one side. Flip and bake 10 minutes on the other side.

Glossary

cuisine: A style of cooking.

culture: A group of people who share beliefs and ways of life.

diverse: Different or varied.

dough: A mix of flour and water.

dumpling: A small ball of dough, sometimes with food inside.

herb: A low-growing plant used to add a taste to food.

import: To buy a good from another country.

ingredient: A part of a mixture.

polenta: Yellow flour made from corn that is cooked with water and sometimes baked or fried.

recipe: An explanation of how to make a food.

region: A large area of land that has features that make it different from nearby areas of land.

specialty: A special skill or creation.

For More Information

Books

Lombardo, Jennifer. *Italy*. Buffalo, NY: Cavendish Square Publishing, 2024.

Redshaw, Hermione. *A Visit to Italy*. Minneapolis, MN: Bearport Publishing, 2024.

Websites

Italy
kids.nationalgeographic.com/geography/countries/article/Italy
Learn more about Italy with National Geographic Kids.

Italy Facts
easyscienceforkids.com/all-about-italy/
Explore fun facts about Italy, including its landmarks and cuisine.

Publisher's note to educators and parents: Our editors have carefully reviewed these websites to ensure that they are suitable for students. Many websites change frequently, however, and we cannot guarantee that a site's future contents will continue to meet our high standards of quality and educational value. Be advised that students should be closely supervised whenever they access the internet.

Index

biscotti, 20, 21
bruschetta, 14
cioppino, 5
Florence, 12
gelato, 20, 21
Lombardy, 10, 11
Milan, 10
Naples, 16, 17
risotto, 10
Rome, 14, 15
Sicily, 18, 19
spaghetti, 7

tomatoes, 6, 8, 9, 10, 14, 16, 17
Tuscany, 12, 13
Umbria, 12, 13
Venice, 11